OCT - 5 2016

D0754394

DISCOVER THE CONTINENTS

South America

by Emily Rose Oachs

BELLWETHER MEDIA · MINNEAPOLIS, MN

BLASTOFF! READERS

3

Note to Librarians, Teachers, and Parents:

Blastoff! Readers are carefully developed by literacy experts and combine standards-based content with developmentally appropriate text.

Level 1 provides the most support through repetition of high-frequency words, light text, predictable sentence patterns, and strong visual support.

Level 2 offers early readers a bit more challenge through varied simple sentences, increased text load, and less repetition of high-frequency words.

Level 3 advances early-fluent readers toward fluency through increased text and concept load, less reliance on visuals, longer sentences, and more literary language.

Level 4 builds reading stamina by providing more text per page, increased use of punctuation, greater variation in sentence patterns, and increasingly challenging vocabulary.

Level 5 encourages children to move from "learning to read" to "reading to learn" by providing even more text, varied writing styles, and less familiar topics.

Whichever book is right for your reader, Blastoff! Readers are the perfect books to build confidence and encourage a love of reading that will last a lifetime!

This edition first published in 2016 by Bellwether Media, Inc.

No part of this publication may be reproduced in whole or in part without written permission of the publisher. For information regarding permission, write to Bellwether Media, Inc., Attention: Permissions Department, 5357 Penn Avenue South, Minneapolis, MN 55419.

Library of Congress Cataloging-in-Publication Data

Oachs, Emily Rose, author.
  South America / by Emily Rose Oachs.
     pages cm. – (Blastoff! Readers: Discover the Continents)
  Includes bibliographical references and index.
  Summary: "Simple text and full-color photography introduce beginning readers to South America. Developed by literacy experts for students in kindergarten through third grade"– Provided by publisher.
  Audience: Grades K-3.
  ISBN 978-1-62617-329-3 (hardcover : alk. paper)
  1. South America–Juvenile literature. I. Title.
  F2208.5.O15 2016
  980–dc23
                                      2015028728

Text copyright © 2016 by Bellwether Media, Inc. BLASTOFF! READERS and associated logos are trademarks and/or registered trademarks of Bellwether Media, Inc. SCHOLASTIC, CHILDREN'S PRESS, and associated logos are trademarks and/or registered trademarks of Scholastic Inc.

Printed in the United States of America, North Mankato, MN.

Table of Contents

Home of the Largest Rain Forest

Amazon
rain forest

South America holds the world's largest **tropical rain forest**. The Amazon spreads across eight countries. Millions of plants and animals live there.

In Peru's mountains, many people visit Machu Picchu's **ruins**. Others travel to Ecuador's Galápagos Islands.

DID YOU KNOW?

- Most people in South America speak Spanish or Portuguese.

- The Andes Mountains stretch for more than 5,000 miles (8,000 kilometers). They are the longest mountain chain on land.

- More than 3,000 types of birds call South America home. Toucans, hummingbirds, parrots, and hawks fly over the land.

- Chile's Atacama Desert is the driest place in the world. There, a city once went without rain for more than 14 years!

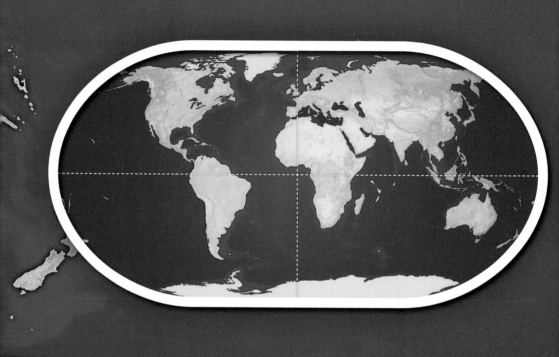

The **equator** passes through South America. The **continent** is in the Northern, Southern, and Western **hemispheres**.

equator

Pacific
Ocean

Atlantic
Ocean

N
W E
S

The Pacific Ocean borders
western South America. To the
east is the Atlantic Ocean. A strip
of land connects South America
to North America.

The Land and Climate

Andes
Mountains

The Andes Mountains trail
along the continent's western
edge. **Volcanoes** rise between
mountain peaks. Low grasslands
spread across Colombia,
Venezuela, and Argentina.

The Amazon River
flows from the Andes
to the Atlantic Ocean.
Around it grows the
Amazon rain forest.

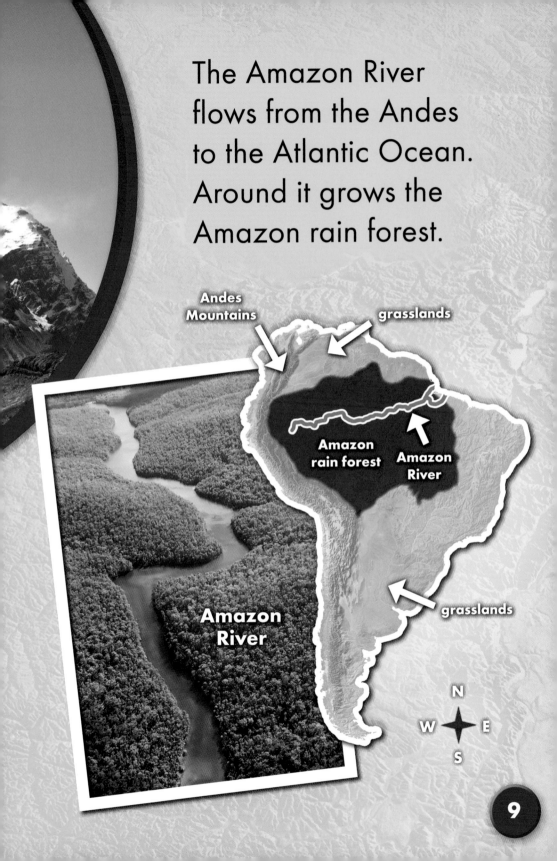

Andes
Mountains

grasslands

Amazon
rain forest

Amazon
River

Amazon
River

grasslands

N
W E
S

West of the Andes lies the Atacama Desert. **Patagonia** covers southern Argentina and Chile. It is high, rocky land.

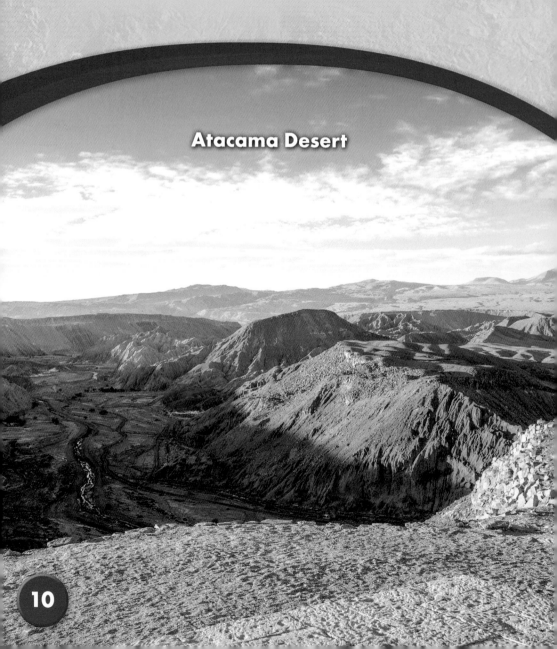

Atacama Desert

Patagonia

Atacama Desert

Patagonia

N
W E
S

Most of the continent's **climate** is **tropical**.
The southern tip is colder.

The Plants and Animals

Brazil nut tree

passionflower

In the Amazon, orchids and vines grow on trees. Passionflowers bloom and bear fruit. Brazil nut trees tower over the rain forest.

Cypress forests appear in the southern Andes. In Argentina, ombu trees dot the grasslands.

ombu tree

cypress forest

Jaguars and spider monkeys roam the Amazon. Poison dart frogs and green anacondas also live there.

spider monkey

poison dart frog

green anaconda

jaguar

guanacos

rockhoppers

Guanacos climb in the Andes. Their cousins, llamas, carry packs for humans. In the far south, rockhoppers and other penguins hunt in the ocean.

About 410 million people call South America home. The continent has 12 countries. Two **territories** are ruled by countries overseas.

Brazil is South America's largest country. It touches every South American country except two. It also has the most people.

Guyana

Suriname

French Guiana (territory)

Venezuela

Colombia

Ecuador

Peru

Brazil

Bolivia

Paraguay

Chile

Argentina

Uruguay

Falkland Islands (territory)

N
W   E
S

Each year, Brazil holds the **festival** *Carnaval*. Parades and music fill the streets. People dance in fancy, colorful costumes.

Brazilians take pride in Carnaval. People work together for months to prepare. In South America, festivals bring people together in work and in play!

Size: 6,878,000 square miles
(17,814,000 square kilometers);
4th largest continent

Number of Countries: 12

Largest Country: Brazil

Smallest Country: Suriname

Number of People: 410 million people

Place with Most People: Brazil

Top Natural Resources: iron, oil, natural gas, gems, wood

Top Landmarks:
- Machu Picchu (Peru)
- Iguazú Falls (Argentina/Brazil)
- Christ the Redeemer statue (Brazil)
- Easter Island (Chile)
- Galápagos Islands (Ecuador)

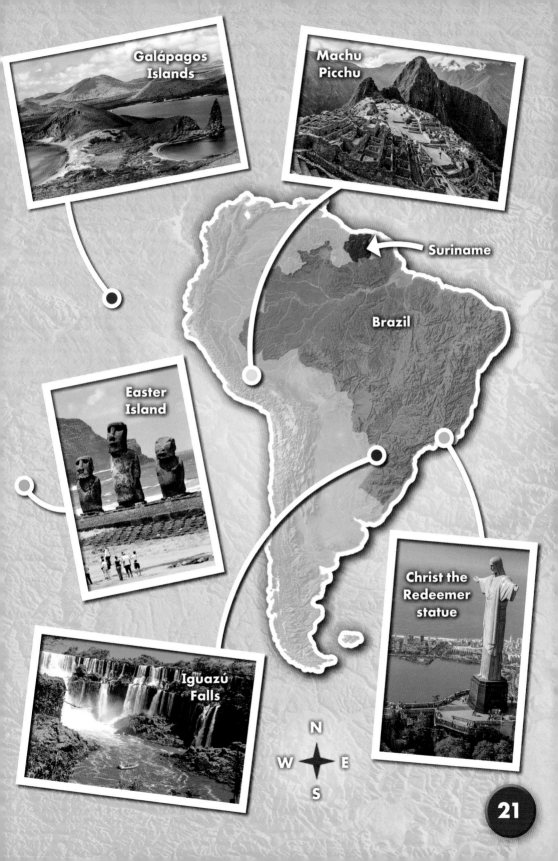

Galápagos Islands

Machu Picchu

Suriname

Brazil

Easter Island

Christ the Redeemer statue

Iguazú Falls

N
W   E
S

Glossary

climate—the weather patterns in an area over a long period of time

continent—one of the seven main land areas on Earth; the continents are Africa, Antarctica, Asia, Australia, Europe, North America, and South America.

equator—an imaginary line around the center of Earth; the equator divides the planet into a northern half and a southern half.

festival—a joyful event to honor a special occasion

hemispheres—halves of the globe; the equator and prime meridian divide Earth into different hemispheres.

Patagonia—the southernmost region of South America; both Chile and Argentina own parts of Patagonia.

ruins—the physical remains of a human-made structure

territories—areas of land that belong to a country

tropical—part of the tropics; the tropics is a hot, rainy region near the equator.

tropical rain forest—a thick, green forest that lies in the hot and wet regions near the equator

volcanoes—holes in the earth; when a volcano erupts, hot, melted rock called lava shoots out.

To Learn More

AT THE LIBRARY
Ganeri, Anita. *Introducing South America*. Chicago, Ill.: Capstone Heinemann Library, 2014.

Kalman, Bobbie. *Spotlight on Brazil*. New York, N.Y.: Crabtree Publishing, 2011.

Rice, William B. *Amazon Rainforest*. Huntington Beach, Calif.: Teacher Created Materials, 2012.

ON THE WEB
Learning more about South America is as easy as 1, 2, 3.

1. Go to www.factsurfer.com.

2. Enter "South America" into the search box.

3. Click the "Surf" button and you will see a list of related web sites.

With factsurfer.com, finding more information is just a click away.

Index

The images in this book are reproduced through the courtesy of: Jess Kraft, front cover, p. 21 (top left, top right); Elena Kalistratova, p. 4; Roberto Tetsuo Okamura, p. 5; kavram, p. 8; Johnny Lye, p. 9; DC_Colombia, p. 10; Pichugin Dmitry, p. 11; Edward Parker/ Alamy, p. 12 (top); cristalvi, p. 12 (bottom); Cienpies Design, p. 13 (top); Christian Handl/ imageBROKER/ Corbis, p. 13 (bottom); Ammit Jack, p. 14 (left); Nazzu, p. 14 (top right); Dirk Ercken, p. 14 (middle right); hin255, p. 14 (bottom right); Anton_Ivanov, p. 15 (top); sunsinger, pp. 15 (bottom), 16; T photography, p. 18; lazyllama, p. 19; Amy Nichole Harris, p. 21 (middle); Det-anan, p. 21 (bottom left); Mark Schwettmann, p. 21 (bottom right).